Signal from the Ninth Horizon

This book provides a practical framework for restoring clarity, unity, and long-term direction in a world overwhelmed by noise, division, and short-term thinking.

By Laura Lee

AF720541

Lauxon Publishing, LLC

Published by Lauxon Publishing, LLC

For permission requests, please contact:
Email: info@Lauxonpublishing.com
Website: www.Lauxonpublishing.com

Author Note

This book emerged from observation, reflection, and lived experience in both creative and digital environments. Working at the intersection of design, strategy, and storytelling has revealed a consistent pattern: systems influence behavior, and behavior influences culture. When systems prioritize engagement over clarity, noise grows. When systems prioritize integrity over speed, signal strengthens.

As a creative entrepreneur, I have seen how intention transforms outcomes. Design is never neutral — it guides perception. Communication is never passive — it shapes reality. The principles in this book are rooted in that understanding: that structure, language, and incentives matter deeply.

Signal from the Ninth Horizon is not meant to provide rigid answers. It is designed as a framework — adaptable, scalable, and applicable across communities, organizations, and personal life. The goal is not perfection, but alignment. Not control, but coherence.

My hope is that readers use this work as both mirror and map: a mirror for reflection, and a map for action.

Table of Contents

Chapter 8: Inner Clarity as Foundation
We establish why personal awareness is the starting point for collective transformation.

Chapter 9: Cognitive Hygiene
We introduce practices for filtering mental noise and strengthening discernment.

Chapter 10: Emotional Regulation in High-Stress Systems
We develop methods for maintaining stability under social and technological pressure.

Chapter 11: Values as Navigation Tools
We define how clearly articulated principles guide consistent and ethical action.

Chapter 12: Purpose-Driven Identity
We explain how aligned identity reduces confusion and increases resilience.

Chapter 13: Reclaiming Focus in a Distracted World
We provide strategies for protecting deep attention and meaningful productivity.

Chapter 14: Building Mental Resilience
We demonstrate how adaptability strengthens both individuals and communities.

Part III: Restoring Social Signal

Chapter 15: Trust as Infrastructure
We argue that trust is the invisible foundation of economic and social stability.

Chapter 16: Transparent Communication Models
We design systems that prioritize clarity, accountability, and verifiable information.

Chapter 17: Constructive Dialogue Frameworks
We outline methods for turning disagreement into innovation rather than division.

Chapter 18: Bridging Ideological Divides
We present tools for finding shared interests across cultural and political boundaries.

Chapter 19: Collaborative Intelligence
We explore how collective problem-solving outperforms isolated expertise.

Chapter 20: Community-Based Decision Making
We show how localized engagement improves legitimacy and effectiveness.

Chapter 21: Reinventing Leadership for the Signal Age
We redefine leadership as signal amplification rather than control.

Part IV: Technological Alignment

Chapter 22: Designing Ethical Systems
We propose principles for building technologies that enhance human capability.

Chapter 23: Algorithmic Responsibility
We call for transparent design in recommendation and information systems.

Chapter 24: Information Verification Ecosystems
We introduce layered validation processes to reduce misinformation.

Chapter 25: Human-Centered Innovation
We advocate for development that prioritizes long-term societal benefit.

Chapter 26: Data with Context
We stress the importance of interpretation frameworks alongside raw data.

Chapter 27: Resilient Digital Communities
We create models for healthy online interaction and sustainable engagement.

Chapter 28: Technology as Amplifier of Wisdom
We reorient innovation toward enhancing discernment and cooperation.

Part V: Economic and Structural Renewal

Chapter 29: Sustainable Economic Indicators
We propose alternative metrics beyond short-term profit.

Chapter 30: Incentive Redesign
We align reward systems with long-term human and environmental well-being.

Chapter 31: Circular Resource Systems
We promote regenerative models that reduce waste and depletion.

Chapter 32: Equitable Opportunity Frameworks
We establish pathways for access, mobility, and participation.

Chapter 33: Localized Resilience Networks
We strengthen regional systems to reduce vulnerability to global shocks.

Chapter 34: Adaptive Governance Models
We design flexible institutions capable of evolving with emerging realities.

Part VI: Global Integration

Chapter 35: Planetary Perspective
We shift from national competition toward shared global stewardship.

Chapter 36: Cross-Cultural Signal Exchange
We develop methods for respectful knowledge sharing across societies.

Chapter 37: Conflict Transformation Systems
We replace adversarial structures with restorative approaches.

Chapter 38: Education for Signal Literacy
We redefine education to include critical thinking, media literacy, and systems awareness.

Chapter 39: Intergenerational Alignment
We prioritize decisions that protect future generations.

Chapter 40: The Ninth Horizon Vision
We synthesize the framework into a unified path forward that restores clarity, cooperation, and sustainable progress.

Prologue

We are living in an age defined not by lack of information, but by excess. Signals arrive faster than we can interpret them, and noise often travels farther than truth. The challenge is no longer access — it is discernment. In a world where attention is constantly requested and rarely restored, clarity has become both rare and revolutionary.

This book was written in response to that condition. It is not a critique of technology, progress, or connectivity. It is an invitation to realign them. The systems shaping our lives are powerful, but they are not fixed. They reflect human choices. And human choices can evolve.

The signal we seek is not external. It begins within awareness, deepens through integrity, and expands through cooperation. When individuals cultivate inner clarity, institutions can reflect transparency. When communication becomes responsible, trust can return. When incentives are redesigned for long-term well-being, stability follows.

The Ninth Horizon represents that forward boundary where vision meets responsibility. It is the point at which we choose coherence over chaos, collaboration over fragmentation, and wisdom over reaction. This book offers a framework for moving toward that horizon — deliberately, practically, and collectively.

The signal is still here. It has not disappeared. It is waiting to be strengthened.

CHAPTER . 1

The Age of Overload

Modern civilization is immersed in an unprecedented flood of information. Messages arrive constantly from devices, platforms, institutions, and peers, each competing for immediate attention. The speed of communication has increased dramatically, while the capacity for reflection has remained biologically limited. As a result, individuals are forced to process more input than the human mind was designed to handle. This imbalance creates cognitive strain that gradually reshapes perception. Over time, overload becomes the baseline condition rather than the exception.

When information exceeds our ability to evaluate it carefully, attention fragments. Decisions become reactive instead of intentional. The mind shifts from deep analysis to rapid scanning, prioritizing novelty over substance. This pattern reduces the quality of judgment in both personal and collective contexts. Short bursts of stimulation replace sustained understanding. In such an environment, clarity struggles to survive.

Information saturation does not merely increase knowledge; it changes behavior. Constant alerts train the nervous system to expect interruption. Focus becomes fragile and easily disrupted by external signals. This condition weakens long-term thinking because sustained concentration is essential for complex reasoning. Without uninterrupted cognitive space, ideas remain incomplete. Consequently, problem-solving capacity declines even as data availability expands.

The overload environment also affects emotional stability. Continuous exposure to intense content elevates stress levels. The brain interprets persistent stimulation as urgency, even when no immediate threat exists. This chronic activation interferes with calm reflection and balanced decision-making. Over time, heightened reactivity becomes normalized. Stability is replaced by continuous alertness.

In a system saturated with input, meaningful patterns become harder to detect. Signal blends with noise, and important information competes with trivial content. The volume of communication obscures its relevance. Individuals may feel informed while actually being overwhelmed. Quantity begins to substitute for quality. The result is a paradox in which access to information increases while understanding diminishes.

Recognizing the condition of overload is the first step toward restoring clarity. Awareness creates the possibility of intentional filtering. Without acknowledgment of the problem, corrective action cannot begin. Overload is not simply a technological issue; it is a structural shift in how society processes reality. Addressing it requires both personal discipline and systemic redesign. The path forward begins with understanding how deeply saturation has reshaped attention itself.

The modern attention environment is engineered for persistence rather than clarity. Platforms are designed to maximize engagement, not understanding. This design encourages continuous interaction through notifications, recommendations, and algorithmic suggestions. Each interaction reinforces the cycle of consumption and response. As engagement increases, reflection decreases. The structure of the system shapes the structure of the mind.

Over time, exposure to constant stimulation alters baseline expectations. Silence begins to feel uncomfortable. Stillness can seem unproductive. The absence of input may even create anxiety because the brain adapts to regular stimulation. This adaptation transforms interruption into normality. What once felt excessive gradually feels necessary.

The consequences extend beyond individual experience into collective behavior. When large populations operate under constant stimulation, public discourse accelerates. Conversations become shorter and more reactive. Complex issues are reduced to simplified messages that fit limited attention windows. Nuance struggles to compete with immediacy. Depth is often replaced by speed.

This acceleration affects institutions as well. Decision cycles shorten in response to public pressure and media dynamics. Leaders may feel compelled to respond instantly rather than thoughtfully. Policy development becomes reactive instead of strategic. Long-term planning loses priority in environments demanding rapid updates. Structural patience becomes increasingly rare.

As overload intensifies, discernment becomes more difficult. Distinguishing credible information from misleading content requires time and cognitive effort. When attention is fragmented, verification processes weaken. People rely more heavily on headlines, summaries, and impressions. This reliance increases vulnerability to distortion. Without deliberate filtering, perception becomes unstable.

Addressing the age of overload requires rebuilding intentional attention practices. Individuals must learn to create boundaries around input streams. Systems must also be redesigned to support clarity rather than exploitation of focus. Restoring balance will not happen automatically. It requires conscious effort at both personal and structural levels. The next step is understanding how signal itself collapses within this environment.

Signal collapses when clarity can no longer compete with volume. In environments dominated by constant input, meaningful information becomes indistinguishable from background noise. The mind struggles to prioritize when everything demands equal urgency. Without hierarchy, evaluation becomes exhausting. Over time, exhaustion replaces discernment. What remains is reaction rather than reflection.

The collapse of signal does not mean truth disappears. Instead, truth becomes harder to identify and verify. Reliable information must now compete with emotionally charged content designed for visibility. Visibility often depends on engagement metrics rather than accuracy. As a result, distortion can spread faster than correction. The speed of amplification exceeds the speed of validation.

This imbalance reshapes trust. When individuals encounter conflicting messages repeatedly, uncertainty grows. Repeated exposure to contradiction weakens confidence in shared facts. Without shared reference points, cooperative action becomes difficult. Trust erodes not because truth vanishes, but because clarity becomes rare. In the absence of stable signal, skepticism becomes default.

The collapse of signal also affects decision quality. When input streams are dominated by urgency and emotion, reasoning processes are bypassed. Immediate responses replace careful analysis. This pattern reduces the ability to evaluate long-term consequences. Decisions made under constant stimulation tend to favor short-term outcomes. Over time, systemic stability is compromised.

Rebuilding signal requires restoring filters at multiple levels. Individuals must cultivate habits that prioritize verification and thoughtful review. Institutions must design communication systems that emphasize accuracy and context. Technology platforms must align incentives with clarity rather than confusion. Without structural adjustment, overload will continue to degrade signal. Restoring balance depends on redefining how information is produced and distributed.

The collapse of signal is not an inevitable outcome of technology itself. It is the result of design choices, incentive structures, and cultural habits. Recognizing this distinction opens the door to change. If systems can amplify noise, they can also amplify clarity. The challenge is to intentionally build environments where signal is stronger than distraction. Understanding this dynamic prepares the foundation for examining attention as a resource.

Attention functions as the primary gateway to experience. Every perception, thought, and decision depends on where attention is directed. In modern systems, attention has become a measurable and monetizable asset. Platforms compete for it because it drives visibility, revenue, and influence. As competition intensifies, strategies evolve to capture and retain focus. This transformation turns human awareness into economic infrastructure.

When attention becomes currency, its allocation reflects market incentives rather than personal intention. Content that provokes strong emotion often receives greater engagement. Sensational material can outperform careful analysis because it generates immediate reactions. Over time, this skews the information environment toward stimulation. Subtlety struggles to compete with intensity. The result is an ecosystem optimized for retention rather than comprehension.

The monetization of attention also shapes behavioral patterns. Users are trained through repetition to scroll, click, and respond. Each interaction provides data that refines future targeting. This feedback loop increases personalization, which can enhance relevance but also narrow perspective. Over-specialization reduces exposure to diverse viewpoints. Limited exposure can weaken critical thinking.

In such a system, distraction becomes profitable. Interruptions generate measurable engagement metrics. Notifications are engineered to create urgency and anticipation. These design elements encourage frequent return rather than sustained engagement. While this increases platform usage, it fragments focus. Fragmented focus reduces the capacity for deep work and long-term planning.

Reclaiming attention requires recognizing its intrinsic value. Attention determines the quality of decisions, relationships, and creative output. When it is scattered, outcomes become inconsistent. When it is directed deliberately, results improve in clarity and effectiveness. Establishing boundaries around attention restores agency. Without intentional control, external systems will continue to define its distribution.

Understanding attention as currency reframes responsibility. Individuals must protect their focus with the same seriousness applied to financial resources. Institutions must evaluate whether their systems support concentration or exploitation. Technology must be assessed by how it influences cognitive well-being. Only by redefining value can attention shift from being consumed to being cultivated. This perspective prepares the ground for examining fragmentation of perspective.

Fragmentation of perspective occurs when individuals consume information within isolated environments. Algorithms personalize content streams to match previous behavior. While personalization increases perceived relevance, it also narrows exposure. Over time, separate information worlds emerge for different groups. Shared reference points diminish. Communication becomes more difficult across boundaries.

When perspectives fragment, consensus becomes harder to achieve. People may interpret the same event through entirely different frameworks. Without common context, disagreement intensifies. Dialogue shifts from exploration to defense. Participants focus on protecting their views rather than understanding others. This dynamic reduces collaborative potential.

Fragmentation also weakens problem-solving capacity. Complex challenges require integrating multiple viewpoints. When information sources remain siloed, synthesis becomes rare. Decisions are made based on partial awareness rather than comprehensive understanding. This limitation increases the risk of unintended consequences. Holistic analysis is replaced by compartmentalized reasoning.

The absence of shared perspective fosters polarization. Groups reinforce internal narratives while dismissing external ones. Repetition within echo environments strengthens conviction. Contradictory information may be filtered out automatically. This selective exposure reduces adaptability. Flexibility declines when exposure is restricted.

Restoring shared perspective requires intentional cross-exposure. Individuals must seek diverse sources of information. Institutions must design platforms that encourage balanced discovery. Education systems must emphasize critical thinking and media literacy. Dialogue spaces must prioritize respectful engagement across differences. Integration of viewpoints strengthens collective intelligence.

Without deliberate effort to bridge perspectives, fragmentation will continue to widen. The solution is not uniformity, but mutual visibility. Understanding differences without hostility enables cooperation. Shared reality does not require identical beliefs. It requires agreement on foundational facts and processes for verification. With this foundation, societies can address deeper systemic challenges, including short-term thinking.

Short-term thinking emerges naturally in environments defined by rapid feedback and constant stimulation. When rewards are immediate, the mind adapts to prioritize what is visible and urgent.

Delayed outcomes receive less cognitive weight because they lack instant reinforcement. Over time, this preference reshapes planning behavior. Long-range strategies compete with near-term impulses. The faster reward typically wins.

Modern information systems amplify this tendency. Metrics update in real time, displaying continuous performance indicators. Social validation arrives through likes, shares, and comments within seconds. This immediate feedback loop strengthens reactive decision-making. Individuals and institutions alike become conditioned to optimize for rapid results. Strategic patience becomes increasingly rare.

Short-term incentives influence organizational structures as well. Quarterly reporting cycles can overshadow multi-year development plans. Leaders may feel pressure to demonstrate immediate progress. Investments that require extended timelines can appear less attractive. This dynamic can discourage foundational improvements. Surface-level gains may be prioritized over structural resilience.

The consequences of short-term orientation accumulate gradually. Deferred maintenance leads to systemic fragility. Environmental impacts may intensify before corrective measures are implemented. Social tensions can deepen when underlying issues are not addressed. Because effects are delayed, responsibility can appear distant. The gap between action and consequence weakens accountability.

Reversing short-term bias requires intentional redesign of incentives. Metrics must incorporate long-term performance indicators. Governance systems should reward sustainable outcomes rather than immediate appearances. Educational approaches should cultivate patience and foresight. Cultural narratives must elevate endurance and stewardship. By aligning rewards with future stability, societies can rebalance their temporal focus.

When short-term thinking dominates, collective capacity diminishes. When long-term vision guides action, resilience increases. Restoring balance between present needs and future responsibilities is essential. Attention systems must support reflection rather than constant reaction. Only then can decisions reflect comprehensive awareness. This understanding leads naturally to examining emotional amplification systems.

Emotional amplification systems arise when platforms and communication channels prioritize content that triggers strong affective responses. Content that evokes anger, fear, or outrage tends to spread rapidly. Emotional intensity increases engagement, and engagement increases visibility. This feedback loop rewards stimulation over balance. As a result, emotionally charged material often outperforms measured analysis. The system gradually selects for intensity.

When emotional triggers dominate information flow, decision-making patterns shift. Individuals exposed to high levels of arousal may respond impulsively. Heightened emotion narrows cognitive processing, reducing openness to alternative perspectives. Complex problems become framed in binary terms. Nuance is replaced by simplified opposition. This dynamic reduces constructive problem-solving capacity.

Outrage-driven environments can distort civic stability. Public discourse becomes reactive and confrontational. Participants may focus on winning arguments rather than understanding issues. Repeated exposure to conflict-oriented messaging increases polarization. Communities begin to organize around emotional alignment instead of shared goals. Cooperative frameworks weaken under sustained emotional pressure.

Emotional amplification also affects perception of risk. Constant exposure to alarming content can inflate perceived threats. When the nervous system remains activated, vigilance becomes chronic. Chronic stress impairs memory, concentration, and patience. Over time, individuals may experience fatigue from continuous concern.

Exhaustion can further reduce the ability to evaluate information carefully.

Reducing the influence of emotional amplification requires structural and personal adjustments. Systems must avoid optimizing solely for engagement metrics. Design choices should prioritize context, accuracy, and constructive dialogue. Individuals can practice intentional consumption habits that limit exposure to destabilizing content. Creating space between stimulus and response restores cognitive control. Stability improves when intensity is balanced with reflection.

By recognizing how emotional systems shape collective behavior, societies can begin to recalibrate communication norms. Encouraging measured discourse supports healthier decision environments. Promoting verification over virality strengthens trust. Emotional awareness combined with structural reform can reduce distortion. With these adjustments, attention regains its capacity to support reasoned judgment. This sets the stage for addressing the loss of shared reality.

The loss of shared reality occurs when communities no longer agree on basic facts, evidence standards, or trusted sources. In fragmented information environments, different groups inhabit distinct interpretive frameworks. Each framework may feel internally consistent, yet externally incompatible. When foundational references diverge, collaboration becomes increasingly difficult. Dialogue shifts from shared exploration to competing narratives. This divergence weakens collective coherence.

Repeated exposure to conflicting claims contributes to uncertainty. When individuals encounter contradiction without reliable resolution, confidence declines. Over time, skepticism may extend beyond specific topics to institutions themselves. Trust erodes when verification processes are unclear or inconsistent. Without agreed-upon methods for evaluating information, disagreement becomes persistent. Stability depends on transparent standards of evidence.

Shared reality does not require uniform opinions. It requires agreement on processes for determining accuracy. When communities recognize common verification principles, disputes can be resolved constructively. Without such principles, debates become unending. The absence of alignment in methodology prevents convergence. Establishing clear criteria for credibility strengthens mutual understanding.

Technology plays a significant role in shaping shared perception. Recommendation systems influence which stories receive attention. Personalization can limit exposure to alternative viewpoints. When exposure narrows, perspective becomes self-reinforcing. Over time, individuals may rarely encounter information outside their established pattern. Reduced cross-exposure intensifies divergence.

Restoring shared reality involves reinforcing transparency and accountability. Information sources must clearly communicate methods and evidence. Institutions should prioritize openness about data and decision processes. Education systems must teach critical evaluation skills. Public dialogue should encourage respectful examination of differing perspectives. These measures support convergence without suppressing diversity.

Recognizing the loss of shared reality is essential for recovery. Without common ground, cooperation weakens across social, political, and economic domains. Rebuilding alignment requires commitment to clarity and verification. By strengthening trust in shared processes, societies can reduce fragmentation. With restored common reference points, collaborative progress becomes achievable. This understanding concludes the first phase of recognizing the noise and prepares the transition toward rebuilding internal signal.

Chapter . 2

The Collapse of Signal

The collapse of signal occurs when accuracy loses priority within communication systems. In environments optimized for speed, information spreads rapidly without sufficient verification. The emphasis shifts from confirming truth to maximizing reach. As transmission accelerates, filtering processes struggle to keep pace. The result is an environment where unverified content circulates widely. Over time, distortion blends seamlessly with legitimate information.

When systems prioritize immediacy, context is often reduced. Messages are shortened to fit attention constraints. Complex explanations are compressed into simplified statements. While brevity can improve accessibility, excessive reduction removes essential nuance. Without context, meaning becomes vulnerable to misinterpretation. Signal weakens when depth is sacrificed for velocity.

The collapse intensifies when feedback mechanisms reward engagement over correctness. Content that provokes strong reactions tends to gain visibility. Accuracy does not always generate rapid interaction. Therefore, systems that rank material by popularity may inadvertently elevate misleading claims. Visibility becomes decoupled from reliability. This structural imbalance amplifies noise.

As signal degrades, collective confidence declines. When audiences repeatedly encounter conflicting information, uncertainty increases. Trust in communicators diminishes if corrections are delayed or unclear. Consistent exposure to ambiguity can produce fatigue. Cognitive overload combines with credibility gaps. Together, these factors erode shared understanding.

Restoring signal requires intentional design adjustments. Verification processes must be integrated into communication pipelines. Transparency regarding sources and evidence strengthens reliability. Platforms and institutions should align incentives with factual integrity. Speed should not override validation. When accuracy is prioritized, clarity becomes sustainable.

The collapse of signal is reversible when systems are redesigned around truth rather than volume. By strengthening verification standards and elevating responsible communication, societies can rebuild stable information pathways. Signal improves when accountability is embedded at every stage of transmission. With reinforced clarity, collaboration becomes more effective. Understanding this dynamic prepares the foundation for examining attention as currency in greater depth.

CHAPTER . 3

Attention as Currency

Attention has become one of the most valuable resources in modern society. Unlike traditional commodities, attention cannot be manufactured or stored. It is finite and renews only through rest and recovery. Every interaction requires a portion of this limited resource. When attention is directed, other possibilities are excluded. Therefore, how attention is allocated determines the quality of experience and outcome.

In digital environments, attention is traded implicitly. Platforms offer free access to services in exchange for user engagement. Revenue models depend on sustained focus. The longer individuals remain engaged, the greater the economic return. This structure incentivizes the design of compelling content. As competition intensifies, techniques for capturing attention become increasingly sophisticated.

When attention functions as currency, its distribution reflects market dynamics. Content that attracts clicks and shares gains prominence. Emotional triggers, novelty, and personalization enhance visibility. However, these features do not always correlate with informational value. As a result, highly engaging material may overshadow more substantive contributions. This imbalance shapes public perception.

The commodification of attention influences individual behavior. Users may feel compelled to remain constantly connected. The expectation of availability creates pressure to respond quickly. Continuous engagement reduces opportunities for deep focus. Over time, fragmented attention becomes habitual. Productivity and reflection both decline when focus is consistently interrupted.

Reclaiming attention requires deliberate boundaries. Structured periods of disconnection support cognitive restoration. Intentional consumption habits improve clarity and reduce overload. Organizations can also redesign workflows to prioritize concentration. Educational systems can teach attention management as a core skill. When attention is treated as a protected asset, its value increases.

Attention determines the direction of thought, action, and culture. If it is scattered, outcomes become inconsistent. If it is directed strategically, progress becomes measurable and sustained. Understanding attention as currency reveals both its vulnerability and its power. Protecting it is essential for restoring signal within society. This awareness transitions naturally into examining the fragmentation of perspective.

CHAPTER . 4

The Fragmentation of Perspective

Fragmentation of perspective occurs when individuals consume information within isolated environments shaped by personalization and algorithmic filtering. These environments gradually limit exposure to alternative viewpoints. As content streams become tailored to prior behavior, experiences grow increasingly similar within each group. Over time, distinct information ecosystems emerge. Each ecosystem reinforces its own interpretations. Shared understanding becomes more difficult to maintain.

When perspectives diverge without cross-exposure, interpretation gaps widen. The same event may generate contrasting conclusions across different communities. Without common reference points, disagreement intensifies. Dialogue shifts from exploration to defense. Participants often focus on validating existing beliefs rather than examining new evidence. This dynamic reduces openness and mutual comprehension.

Fragmentation affects problem-solving capacity. Complex challenges require integrating multiple perspectives and disciplines. When exposure remains narrow, synthesis becomes limited. Decisions are then based on partial information. Partial awareness increases the risk of unintended consequences. Comprehensive solutions become harder to construct.

Polarization can grow in fragmented environments. Repeated interaction with similar viewpoints strengthens internal confidence. Contradictory information may be dismissed or ignored. This reinforcement cycle deepens divisions between groups. As divisions expand, trust declines. Reduced trust makes cooperation more difficult.

Addressing fragmentation requires intentional diversification of information sources. Individuals can seek content that challenges assumptions in constructive ways. Institutions can design systems that encourage balanced exposure. Educational programs can emphasize critical thinking and respectful dialogue. Platforms can incorporate mechanisms that promote context and credibility. Cross-perspective engagement strengthens collective intelligence.

Fragmentation is not permanent, but it requires deliberate effort to reverse. Restoring shared understanding depends on transparency, dialogue, and verification. When communities actively bridge informational divides, collaboration improves. Diversity of thought becomes an asset rather than a barrier. With aligned standards for evaluating information, societies can rebuild coherence. This understanding leads to examining the crisis of short-term thinking.

Fragmentation deepens when social incentives reward alignment over exploration. Individuals may feel pressure to conform to group narratives to maintain belonging. Social validation often depends on visible agreement. This dynamic discourages open inquiry across boundaries. Over time, intellectual curiosity can diminish. Identity becomes closely tied to viewpoint.

Digital architecture accelerates this process through recommendation systems. These systems analyze behavior and predict preferences. While personalization improves efficiency, it also reduces randomness in exposure. Reduced randomness limits encounters with unfamiliar ideas. Without exposure to difference, cognitive flexibility declines. Perspective narrows as repetition increases.

The consequences extend into public discourse. Conversations may become echo chambers where similar opinions circulate repeatedly. In such spaces, dissenting voices can appear amplified or alien. Misunderstandings escalate due to limited shared context. Constructive dialogue requires common ground, which becomes harder to establish. Communication loses integrative capacity.

Fragmentation also impacts institutional cooperation. Agencies, organizations, and communities may operate within separate informational frameworks. When data sources differ, interpretations can conflict. Without transparent standards, reconciliation becomes complex. Coordination depends on mutual visibility of evidence and reasoning. Shared methodology supports alignment across sectors.

Rebuilding perspective requires intentional integration. Cross-disciplinary collaboration strengthens understanding of complex systems. Structured dialogue formats can reduce reactive exchanges. Education can emphasize systems thinking and media literacy. Technology can be designed to promote balanced discovery. By encouraging constructive exposure, fragmentation can gradually decrease.

Restoring integrated perspective does not require uniform agreement. It requires shared commitment to verification and respectful engagement. When communities prioritize clarity over division, cooperation improves. Diverse viewpoints can coexist within a stable framework of facts. This stability enables collective progress. The next challenge involves addressing the crisis of short-term thinking in greater depth.

Chapter . 5

The Crisis of Short-Term Thinking

Short-term thinking arises when systems consistently reward immediate outcomes over long-range planning. In environments driven by rapid feedback, present results often overshadow future consequences. This orientation shapes behavior at both individual and institutional levels. When incentives favor quick gains, patience becomes less common. Strategic depth can be replaced by tactical reaction. Over time, this pattern alters cultural priorities.

Modern communication technologies intensify this tendency. Real-time metrics display instant performance indicators. Continuous updates create expectations of immediate progress. Leaders and organizations may feel compelled to respond quickly to public signals. Decisions made under time pressure often prioritize visibility. Long-term stability can receive less attention than short-term approval.

Economic structures can also reinforce short horizons. Reporting cycles frequently emphasize quarterly performance. Investments requiring extended timelines may appear less attractive. Projects that build resilience can be undervalued if returns are delayed. This bias affects infrastructure, education, and environmental stewardship. The cumulative effect increases systemic vulnerability.

Short-term focus influences personal decision-making as well. Instant gratification is easily accessible in digital environments.

Entertainment, shopping, and social validation are available on demand. Immediate rewards can overshadow sustained effort. Goals that require discipline and endurance may feel less compelling. Over time, this dynamic weakens perseverance.

The consequences of short-term orientation accumulate gradually. Deferred maintenance leads to structural weaknesses. Environmental degradation may intensify before corrective measures take effect. Social issues can deepen when underlying causes are not addressed. Because outcomes unfold slowly, responsibility may seem distant. Yet delayed impact does not reduce eventual consequence.

Rebalancing temporal focus requires aligning incentives with long-term outcomes. Institutions can integrate future-oriented metrics into evaluation systems. Educational frameworks can emphasize foresight and delayed gratification. Cultural narratives can highlight stewardship and continuity. Individuals can practice planning methods that incorporate extended time horizons. When present action is evaluated alongside future impact, decision quality improves. This understanding prepares the transition to examining emotional amplification systems in broader context.

CHAPTER . 6

Emotional Amplification Systems

Emotional amplification systems are communication environments designed to prioritize content that generates strong affective responses. These systems operate through algorithms that measure engagement signals such as clicks, comments, shares, and viewing time. Content that triggers intense reactions often receives greater distribution. As amplification increases visibility, emotional intensity becomes a competitive advantage. Over time, the information landscape shifts toward stimulation rather than balance.

When emotional triggers dominate circulation, cognitive processing can narrow. Heightened emotional states influence perception and judgment. Individuals may interpret information through immediate reaction instead of careful analysis. Complex topics can be reduced to simplified emotional frames. This reduction limits nuanced understanding. As nuance declines, polarization becomes more likely.

Outrage, fear, and moral indignation are particularly effective at capturing attention. These emotions create urgency, which increases engagement metrics. Systems that reward engagement inadvertently reward intensity. This feedback loop reinforces the production of emotionally charged material. Balanced or measured content may struggle to achieve similar reach. The structural incentives shape public discourse.

Persistent exposure to amplified emotion affects collective stability. Continuous stimulation can elevate stress levels across populations. Heightened stress reduces patience and increases reactivity. In such conditions, constructive dialogue becomes more difficult. Disagreements escalate quickly. Cooperation requires calm cognitive space, which may be limited in highly amplified environments.

Addressing emotional amplification requires design adjustments. Platforms can incorporate features that promote context alongside engagement. Transparency in algorithmic ranking can help users understand why content appears. Metrics can include indicators of credibility and constructive contribution. Systems can be evaluated not only by growth but also by societal impact. When design aligns with stability, amplification can support clarity rather than distortion.

Reducing excessive emotional escalation strengthens decision-making processes. Balanced communication environments encourage reflection before response. When emotion is integrated with reason, understanding improves. Stability increases when intensity is moderated by verification. Recognizing amplification patterns allows societies to recalibrate information flow. This awareness leads naturally to examining the loss of shared reality in greater depth.

CHAPTER . 7

The Loss of Shared Reality

The loss of shared reality occurs when communities no longer rely on common standards for evaluating facts and evidence. In such environments, information streams diverge into separate interpretive worlds. Each group may possess internally consistent narratives, yet these narratives may conflict with one another. Without overlapping reference points, coordination becomes increasingly difficult. Dialogue shifts from shared inquiry to parallel monologues. Collective decision-making weakens under these conditions.

When shared standards erode, trust declines. Trust depends on confidence that others are operating from comparable evidence and verification processes. If those processes differ, uncertainty grows. Repeated exposure to conflicting claims without resolution intensifies doubt. Over time, skepticism can extend beyond specific topics to institutions and communication channels. Stability requires confidence in methods of validation.

Technology contributes to this divergence by personalizing information exposure. Recommendation systems prioritize content aligned with prior engagement patterns. While personalization increases relevance, it can reduce exposure to alternative viewpoints. Limited cross-exposure narrows interpretive flexibility. Individuals may rarely encounter information outside their established framework. As exposure shrinks, perception becomes more segmented.

The absence of shared reality affects cooperation across social and political domains. Complex challenges demand coordinated responses grounded in common understanding. When foundational facts are disputed, collaboration slows. Energy is diverted toward debate over basic premises. Productive problem-solving requires alignment on evidence before strategy can proceed. Without that alignment, progress becomes fragmented.

Rebuilding shared reality requires transparent standards for verification. Sources must clearly communicate methodologies and evidence bases. Educational systems should emphasize critical evaluation skills and media literacy. Public institutions can reinforce accountability through openness and documentation. Dialogue spaces can encourage respectful examination of differing perspectives. Shared processes, rather than uniform opinions, form the backbone of stability.

The loss of shared reality is not irreversible. When communities recommit to clarity and verification, convergence becomes possible. Agreement on how truth is assessed strengthens collective resilience. Shared standards enable constructive disagreement without destabilization. With common reference points restored, societies can move toward rebuilding internal signal and strengthening individual clarity. This transition opens the path to deeper personal reconstruction.

CHAPTER . 8

Inner Clarity as Foundation

Inner clarity begins with the recognition that external noise cannot be controlled entirely, but internal response can be shaped intentionally. In environments saturated with information, the mind requires structured reflection to maintain stability. Without deliberate awareness, reactions can become automatic. Automatic responses often reflect external stimuli rather than personal values. Developing clarity restores conscious agency. Agency is the basis of meaningful change.

Personal awareness acts as the primary filter for incoming information. When individuals understand their cognitive patterns, they can better evaluate influences. Self-observation reduces impulsive decision-making. It creates space between stimulus and response. That space allows thoughtful consideration. Thoughtful consideration improves judgment quality.

Clarity also depends on emotional awareness. Emotions provide valuable signals about needs and boundaries. However, unexamined emotions can distort perception. Recognizing emotional states helps prevent overreaction. Naming feelings reduces their unconscious control. Emotional literacy strengthens internal stability.

Internal clarity requires alignment between beliefs, actions, and values. When behavior conflicts with principles, cognitive tension arises. Sustained misalignment can reduce confidence and focus. Alignment simplifies decision-making because it provides consistent criteria. Clear principles act as reference points. Reference points reduce ambiguity during uncertainty.

Developing clarity involves structured practices. Reflection, journaling, and mindful pauses can enhance awareness. Limiting exposure to unnecessary stimulation supports mental organization. Intentional routines protect cognitive energy. Consistency in habits reinforces stability. Over time, these practices strengthen resilience.

Inner clarity does not isolate individuals from society. Instead, it prepares them for constructive engagement. A stable internal foundation improves communication and collaboration. When people operate from clarity rather than confusion, interactions become more productive. Collective transformation begins with individual awareness. This foundation supports the next step: establishing cognitive hygiene.

CHAPTER . 9

Cognitive Hygiene

Cognitive hygiene refers to the intentional maintenance of mental environments to reduce distortion and enhance clarity. Just as physical hygiene protects the body, cognitive hygiene protects attention and thought processes. In information-rich systems, mental inputs accumulate quickly. Without regular filtering, irrelevant or misleading material can dominate perception. Structured review helps maintain intellectual cleanliness. Clean input improves decision quality.

The first principle of cognitive hygiene is selective exposure. Not all information requires equal attention. Prioritizing credible and relevant sources reduces unnecessary cognitive load. Curating inputs prevents overwhelm and fragmentation. Intentional selection strengthens focus. Focus enables deeper comprehension.

Verification is another essential component. Accepting claims without evaluation increases vulnerability to error. Cross-referencing information with reliable references strengthens accuracy. Questioning assumptions improves reasoning. Fact-checking habits reduce the spread of distortion. Consistent verification reinforces trust in conclusions.

Cognitive hygiene also involves emotional regulation during information consumption. Strong emotional reactions can impair critical thinking. Pausing before responding allows reflection to intervene. Delaying reaction reduces impulsive sharing.

Thoughtful engagement lowers the amplification of misinformation. Emotional awareness enhances discernment.

Limiting continuous stimulation supports cognitive recovery. Periods of rest allow memory consolidation and integration of ideas. Constant input prevents mental organization. Scheduled breaks restore processing capacity. Silence and reflection improve insight. Recovery is not inactivity but essential maintenance.

Practicing cognitive hygiene strengthens resilience in complex environments. Clear thinking reduces susceptibility to manipulation. Structured habits build intellectual discipline. Over time, these practices improve judgment and stability. Cognitive clarity supports both personal growth and social contribution. This foundation prepares for developing emotional regulation in high-stress systems.

CHAPTER . 10

Emotional Regulation in High-Stress Systems

Emotional regulation is the capacity to maintain stability when exposed to intense or prolonged stimulation. In high-stress information environments, individuals encounter continuous alerts, urgent messaging, and emotionally charged content. Without regulation, these inputs can elevate physiological arousal. Sustained arousal narrows attention and increases reactivity. Over time, chronic stress can impair reasoning. Stability depends on the ability to return to equilibrium.

Regulation begins with awareness of internal states. Recognizing early signs of stress allows for timely intervention. Physical cues such as rapid breathing or muscle tension signal activation. Identifying these signals creates an opportunity for adjustment. Awareness transforms automatic reaction into conscious choice. Conscious choice restores balance.

Breathing techniques, structured pauses, and deliberate reflection can reduce heightened arousal. These practices slow the nervous system's stress response. Slowing down supports clearer thinking. Clarity improves communication and reduces misunderstandings. Calm responses are more likely to produce constructive outcomes. Regulation strengthens both individual performance and collective dialogue.

In organizational contexts, emotional regulation supports effective leadership. Leaders who model composure influence group dynamics positively. Stable behavior reduces uncertainty during complex situations. Teams operating under steady guidance tend to coordinate more effectively. Emotional stability enhances trust. Trust improves cooperation in demanding conditions.

Digital environments can intensify emotional exposure through rapid feedback loops. Continuous engagement may amplify both positive and negative emotions. Without boundaries, individuals can experience fatigue from constant stimulation. Establishing limits on exposure reduces strain. Structured disengagement allows recovery. Balance between engagement and rest is essential.

Emotional regulation is not suppression of feeling but integration of emotion and reason. Healthy systems acknowledge emotional data while preventing impulsive action. When emotion informs rather than controls decisions, outcomes improve. Stability in high-stress systems depends on this integration. With emotional equilibrium strengthened, attention can be redirected toward values as navigation tools.

CHAPTER . 11

Values as Navigation Tools

Values function as internal navigation systems that guide decisions in complex environments. When external information is overwhelming or contradictory, values provide consistent direction. They reduce uncertainty by offering clear criteria for action. Without defined values, choices become reactive and situational. With articulated principles, behavior becomes coherent. Coherence strengthens integrity and trust.

Clearly identified values simplify decision-making. Instead of evaluating every situation from scratch, individuals can compare options against established standards. This reduces cognitive load. It also increases consistency across time. Consistency builds reliability in both personal and professional contexts. Reliability strengthens relationships and reputation.

Values also provide resilience during uncertainty. When external conditions change rapidly, stable principles prevent drift. They anchor behavior amid shifting circumstances. This anchoring reduces susceptibility to manipulation. External pressures lose influence when internal standards are strong. Steadfast values support independence of thought.

In organizational systems, shared values improve alignment. When teams agree on core principles, coordination becomes more efficient. Conflicts are easier to resolve when guided by common standards. Decision-making gains transparency. Transparency enhances accountability. Accountability reinforces collective trust.

Values must be intentionally clarified rather than assumed. Implicit beliefs can remain unexamined and inconsistent. Articulating principles transforms them into conscious commitments. Written and discussed values increase awareness. Awareness allows evaluation of alignment between belief and action. Alignment reduces internal tension.

Using values as navigation tools does not eliminate complexity. Instead, it provides structure within complexity. When decisions are evaluated through stable principles, clarity increases. Stability of direction improves long-term outcomes. With values established as internal guidance, the next step involves cultivating purpose-driven identity.

Chapter . 12

Purpose-Driven Identity

Purpose-driven identity forms when personal meaning aligns with deliberate contribution. In environments filled with distraction, identity can become shaped by external validation rather than internal conviction. Social metrics, trends, and comparisons may influence self-perception. When identity depends primarily on external feedback, stability decreases. Purpose restores internal coherence. Coherence strengthens resilience.

Purpose provides direction during uncertainty. When challenges arise, individuals grounded in purpose can evaluate options more clearly. Purpose narrows focus toward meaningful objectives. It reduces confusion by clarifying priorities. Decisions become easier when aligned with a defined mission. Clarity of intention improves consistency of action.

A purpose-driven identity reduces vulnerability to manipulation. External systems often attempt to shape behavior through emotional triggers or social pressure. When individuals understand their deeper motivations, they are less likely to react impulsively. Purpose acts as an internal filter. It distinguishes between distraction and meaningful engagement. This filtering strengthens autonomy.

Identity grounded in purpose also enhances persistence. Long-term goals require sustained effort. Without meaning, motivation can fade quickly. Purpose provides emotional reinforcement during setbacks. It connects daily tasks to broader outcomes. This connection sustains commitment over time.

Developing purpose requires reflection and honest assessment. Individuals must examine strengths, values, and aspirations. Identifying areas of contribution creates alignment between capability and action. Writing down goals increases clarity. Revisiting those goals reinforces focus. Consistent review ensures ongoing alignment.

Purpose-driven identity does not isolate individuals from society. Instead, it encourages constructive participation. When people act from clear intention, collaboration improves. Purpose aligns personal growth with collective benefit. Stability within the individual contributes to stability within the system. With identity strengthened, the next focus becomes reclaiming focus in a distracted world.

CHAPTER . 13

Reclaiming Focus in a Distracted World

Reclaiming focus requires recognizing distraction as a structural condition rather than a personal failure. Modern environments are intentionally designed to capture and redirect attention. Notifications, infinite scrolling, and algorithmic recommendations continuously compete for mental resources. Without deliberate boundaries, focus fragments into short intervals. Sustained concentration becomes rare. Rebuilding it demands intentional practice.

Deep focus is essential for complex thinking and creative problem-solving. Meaningful progress often depends on uninterrupted engagement with a task. When attention is repeatedly divided, cognitive depth decreases. Fragmented effort produces surface-level outcomes. In contrast, extended concentration enables integration of ideas. Integration leads to insight.

Protecting focus begins with controlling inputs. Limiting unnecessary alerts reduces interruptions. Establishing dedicated time blocks for concentrated work supports mental stability. Creating environments with minimal distractions improves efficiency. Structured routines strengthen consistency. Consistency reinforces neural pathways associated with sustained attention.

Digital consumption habits significantly influence focus capacity. Continuous multitasking trains the brain to expect frequent switching. Task switching increases cognitive fatigue. Fatigue reduces both accuracy and speed. Reducing simultaneous inputs improves mental endurance. Endurance supports long-term productivity.

Rest is also a critical component of focus recovery. The brain requires periods of disengagement to consolidate information. Sleep, reflection, and quiet time restore processing power. Recovery enhances memory and reasoning. Without rest, attention gradually declines. Sustainable focus depends on balance between effort and restoration.

Reclaiming focus is not about rejecting technology but about using it intentionally. Tools should serve defined purposes rather than dictate behavior. Clear priorities guide technology usage. When attention is protected, output improves in quality and depth. Focus strengthens both individual achievement and collective progress. With focus stabilized, attention turns toward building mental resilience.

CHAPTER . 14

Building Mental Resilience

Mental resilience is the capacity to adapt effectively to change, stress, and uncertainty while maintaining psychological stability. In rapidly shifting information environments, resilience enables individuals to process challenges without becoming overwhelmed. It supports recovery after setbacks. It also strengthens the ability to maintain clarity under pressure. Without resilience, stress accumulates. With resilience, growth becomes possible through difficulty.

Resilience begins with cognitive flexibility. Flexible thinking allows individuals to reassess situations when new information emerges. Rigid assumptions can limit adaptation. By remaining open to revision, people improve their problem-solving capacity. Adaptability does not mean instability. It means responsiveness grounded in core values.

Emotional regulation contributes significantly to resilience. The ability to observe feelings without being controlled by them enhances stability. Emotional awareness reduces impulsive reactions. When emotions are acknowledged and processed constructively, they lose destabilizing power. Balanced emotional processing strengthens long-term well-being. Stability supports sustained engagement in complex tasks.

Resilient individuals also cultivate supportive environments. Social connection provides perspective and encouragement during challenges. Collaborative relationships distribute cognitive and emotional load. Community reduces isolation during stress. Shared problem-solving increases confidence. Strong networks enhance recovery and innovation.

Physical health directly influences mental resilience. Adequate sleep, nutrition, and exercise improve cognitive performance. The mind and body operate as an integrated system. When physical systems are supported, psychological endurance increases. Neglecting physical well-being weakens focus and mood. Comprehensive self-care reinforces resilience.

Building mental resilience is an ongoing process rather than a fixed achievement. It develops through practice, reflection, and adjustment. Challenges can serve as opportunities for strengthening adaptive capacity. Each recovery builds confidence in future response. Over time, resilience becomes a stable trait. With resilience established, attention shifts toward restoring social signal in broader systems.

CHAPTER . 15

Trust as Infrastructure

Trust functions as the invisible infrastructure that supports every stable society. It enables cooperation without constant verification. When trust is present, transactions, communication, and collaboration occur efficiently. When trust declines, systems require increased oversight and control. Excessive verification slows progress. Sustainable trust reduces friction and strengthens coordination.

Trust is built through consistency. Repeated alignment between words and actions reinforces credibility. Transparency in processes strengthens confidence. When institutions clearly communicate intentions and outcomes, uncertainty decreases. Predictability encourages engagement. Reliability forms the foundation of long-term relationships.

In economic systems, trust reduces transaction costs. Parties are more willing to collaborate when expectations are clear. Contracts and regulations help formalize trust where necessary. However, overreliance on enforcement can signal low confidence. Balanced systems combine accountability with mutual belief. Stability increases when integrity is culturally reinforced.

Digital environments influence trust at scale. Rapid information flow can both strengthen and undermine credibility. Verification mechanisms help maintain confidence in shared information. Without clear standards, misinformation spreads quickly. Restoring trust requires consistent application of evidence-based practices. Transparency in data handling further reinforces reliability.

Trust also depends on fairness. Perceived inequities weaken confidence in systems and institutions. Equitable processes increase willingness to participate. Inclusive decision-making strengthens legitimacy. When stakeholders feel represented, cooperation improves. Fairness sustains long-term engagement.

Recognizing trust as infrastructure reframes it as a resource requiring maintenance. It must be intentionally cultivated and protected. Systems designed for clarity and accountability reinforce social stability. Without trust, complexity becomes difficult to manage. With trust, societies can coordinate effectively even under uncertainty. This understanding leads to examining transparent communication models.

Chapter . 16

Transparent Communication Models

Transparent communication models prioritize clarity, accessibility, and accountability in the exchange of information. Transparency reduces uncertainty by making sources, methods, and intentions visible. When communication processes are open, trust increases. Stakeholders can evaluate information based on evidence rather than assumptions. Openness strengthens credibility. Credibility enhances cooperation.

Clear documentation is a central element of transparency. When decisions are recorded and explanations are provided, misunderstandings decrease. Accessible language improves comprehension across diverse audiences. Avoiding unnecessary complexity supports inclusion. Information that is understandable is more likely to be accurately interpreted. Comprehension reduces conflict.

Transparency also involves acknowledging limitations. Honest communication includes uncertainty when it exists. Admitting incomplete knowledge prevents overconfidence. Clear statements about confidence levels improve decision quality. When uncertainty is visible, expectations become realistic. Realism strengthens resilience during change.

Verification mechanisms enhance transparent systems. Providing references, data sources, and methodological explanations allows independent review. Independent review reinforces integrity. When findings can be examined publicly, reliability increases. Accountability discourages manipulation. Structured openness promotes long-term stability.

Digital communication platforms can integrate transparency features. Labeling automated content, clarifying algorithmic influence, and explaining recommendation criteria build user awareness. Visibility into system design reduces suspicion. Understanding how information is curated strengthens informed engagement. Transparent architecture supports informed choice. Informed choice enhances agency.

Transparent communication models do not eliminate disagreement, but they reduce confusion. When processes are clear, debates focus on substance rather than speculation. Clarity improves problem-solving efficiency. Shared understanding accelerates collaboration. With transparency established, attention turns toward constructive dialogue frameworks.

CHAPTER . 17

Constructive Dialogue Frameworks

Constructive dialogue frameworks are structured approaches to communication that prioritize understanding over confrontation. In complex societies, disagreements are inevitable. However, the method used to engage disagreement determines whether outcomes are productive or divisive. When dialogue is guided by mutual respect and clarity, differences can lead to innovation. Without structure, conversations may devolve into competition. Frameworks provide that structure.

Effective dialogue begins with active listening. Listening with the intention to understand reduces misinterpretation. When participants accurately reflect each other's perspectives, trust increases. Clarification questions prevent assumptions. Assumptions often escalate conflict unnecessarily. Careful listening creates shared comprehension.

Neutral language supports constructive engagement. Emotionally charged wording can intensify defensiveness. By using precise and balanced terminology, participants lower resistance. Clarity in expression reduces ambiguity. Reduced ambiguity improves alignment. Alignment enables progress toward solutions.

Structured dialogue often includes agreed-upon rules of engagement. Time limits, turn-taking protocols, and fact-checking procedures maintain order. These guidelines ensure that all voices are heard. Equal participation enhances legitimacy. Legitimacy increases willingness to cooperate. Organized conversation reduces chaos.

Constructive frameworks emphasize common goals. Identifying shared interests shifts focus from opposition to collaboration. Even opposing groups may agree on broader objectives. Highlighting overlap fosters unity. Unity does not eliminate difference but integrates it. Integration strengthens collective problem-solving capacity.

Dialogue frameworks are especially important in high-stress environments. When tensions rise, structured methods prevent escalation. Calm facilitation supports balanced participation. Mediation techniques can help reconcile perspectives. By channeling disagreement productively, systems transform conflict into insight. With dialogue strengthened, the next step is bridging ideological divides.

Chapter . 18

Bridging Ideological Divides

Bridging ideological divides requires recognizing that disagreement often stems from differing experiences, priorities, and value interpretations rather than from fundamental incompatibility. In fragmented environments, individuals are frequently exposed only to perspectives that reinforce their existing views. This reinforcement can harden assumptions over time. When assumptions solidify, dialogue becomes more difficult. Constructive engagement depends on openness to alternative frameworks. Openness reduces defensive responses.

The first step in bridging divides is establishing shared facts. Agreement on verifiable information provides a stable foundation for discussion. Without common reference points, conversations drift into parallel narratives. Clear evidence standards help prevent confusion. Transparent sources strengthen credibility across groups. Shared verification processes enable productive comparison of ideas.

Empathy plays a central role in reducing ideological distance. Understanding the reasoning behind another viewpoint does not require adopting it. It involves recognizing the underlying concerns that shape beliefs. Many disagreements are rooted in fears about security, fairness, or opportunity. Identifying these motivations reveals potential areas of overlap. Empathy transforms opposition into inquiry.

Bridging efforts benefit from focusing on shared goals rather than contested labels. When participants identify mutual interests, collaboration becomes more achievable. Practical cooperation on common challenges builds trust incrementally. Success in small joint projects can reduce suspicion. Gradual cooperation establishes patterns of reliability. Reliability supports long-term reconciliation.

Communication strategies also matter. Neutral framing, respectful tone, and precise language reduce escalation. Avoiding exaggeration and mischaracterization helps maintain credibility. Structured dialogue formats encourage balanced participation. Moderated discussions prevent dominance by extreme voices. Orderly engagement creates space for thoughtful exchange.

Bridging ideological divides is not about eliminating differences. Diversity of thought can strengthen collective intelligence when managed constructively. The objective is integration, not uniformity. Integration allows distinct perspectives to contribute to shared solutions. With bridges established between viewpoints, attention can shift toward collaborative intelligence.

CHAPTER . 19

Collaborative Intelligence

Collaborative intelligence emerges when groups combine diverse knowledge, skills, and perspectives to solve problems more effectively than any individual could alone. Complex challenges often exceed the capacity of isolated expertise. When information is shared openly and respectfully, solutions become more robust. Integration of viewpoints reduces blind spots. Collective reasoning strengthens outcomes. Cooperation multiplies capability.

Effective collaboration requires psychological safety. Participants must feel confident that their contributions will be heard without ridicule or dismissal. When people fear negative consequences for sharing ideas, innovation declines. Supportive environments encourage experimentation. Experimentation leads to discovery. Trust within teams enhances creativity.

Clear communication structures improve collaborative efficiency. Defined roles, shared objectives, and transparent processes reduce confusion. Alignment around common goals keeps efforts coordinated. Documentation ensures continuity over time. Structured interaction prevents duplication of effort. Organization transforms collective potential into tangible results.

Technology can support collaborative intelligence when designed appropriately. Shared digital workspaces allow real-time cooperation. Open data platforms enable broader participation in analysis. However, tools must prioritize accuracy and accessibility.

Systems that amplify misinformation undermine collaboration. Responsible design strengthens cooperative outcomes.

Diversity enhances collaborative intelligence when combined with mutual respect. Different backgrounds contribute unique insights. Variation in perspective improves problem-solving breadth. Inclusion expands the range of potential solutions. Constructive integration of differences increases adaptability. Adaptability is essential in changing environments.

Collaborative intelligence represents a shift from competition toward coordination. While healthy competition can inspire innovation, excessive rivalry reduces information sharing. Balanced systems encourage both individual initiative and group alignment. When cooperation is structured effectively, outcomes improve across domains. With collaboration strengthened, the focus turns toward community-based decision making.

CHAPTER . 20

Community-Based Decision Making

Community-based decision making emphasizes participation, transparency, and local engagement in shaping outcomes that affect collective life. When decisions are made closer to the people impacted by them, accountability increases. Local involvement improves contextual understanding. Those directly affected by policies can contribute practical insight. This proximity enhances relevance. Relevance strengthens legitimacy.

Inclusive participation ensures that diverse perspectives are considered. Broader input reduces the risk of overlooking important factors. Structured forums allow community members to express concerns and propose solutions. Open discussions encourage shared responsibility. Shared responsibility increases commitment to outcomes. Commitment improves implementation success.

Clear processes are essential for effective community decision making. Defined procedures prevent confusion about how input translates into action. Transparency about timelines and criteria builds confidence. When participants understand the pathway from discussion to decision, trust grows. Predictable systems reduce frustration. Predictability supports sustained engagement.

Technology can facilitate community involvement through accessible platforms. Digital tools enable wider participation, especially when physical attendance is limited. However, equitable access must be ensured to prevent exclusion. User-friendly interfaces promote broader engagement. Secure systems protect integrity. Responsible implementation enhances participation without compromising reliability.

Community-based approaches often improve adaptability. Local decision-makers can respond quickly to changing conditions. Feedback loops allow for continuous refinement. Adjustments based on real-world outcomes strengthen effectiveness. Iterative processes encourage learning. Learning enhances resilience.

When communities share responsibility for decisions, social cohesion increases. Collective involvement fosters ownership of outcomes. Ownership encourages cooperative problem-solving. Engagement builds stronger networks of trust and communication. With community decision structures reinforced, the next step is redefining leadership for the signal age.

CHAPTER . 21

Reinventing Leadership for the Signal Age

Leadership in the signal age must prioritize clarity, integrity, and amplification of accurate information rather than control or dominance. Traditional leadership models often emphasize authority and hierarchy. While structure remains important, modern complexity requires adaptive guidance. Leaders must navigate rapid change and information saturation. Effective leadership strengthens signal within systems. Signal amplification improves collective understanding.

Signal-age leaders focus on enabling others rather than centralizing decision-making. Empowerment increases distributed intelligence. When individuals are equipped with information and responsibility, systems become more resilient. Decentralized competence reduces bottlenecks. Shared leadership models encourage collaboration. Collaboration enhances innovation and responsiveness.

Transparency is a core leadership principle in high-information environments. Open communication about goals, constraints, and decisions builds trust. Concealing information can create suspicion and confusion. Clear explanations reduce misinterpretation. Accountability reinforces credibility. Credibility sustains long-term influence.

Adaptive leadership is essential in rapidly evolving contexts. Leaders must be willing to revise strategies when evidence changes. Flexibility demonstrates responsiveness rather than inconsistency. Learning-oriented leadership encourages experimentation and feedback. Continuous improvement strengthens organizational performance. Adaptation ensures relevance over time.

Ethical grounding distinguishes signal-age leadership from reactive authority. Decisions should align with defined values and long-term objectives. Short-term popularity should not override foundational principles. Integrity maintains stability during uncertainty. Consistent ethical behavior reinforces institutional trust. Trust enables cooperation across diverse stakeholders.

Reinventing leadership means shifting from command to coordination, from control to clarity, and from amplification of noise to amplification of truth. Leaders become stewards of information quality. They cultivate environments where constructive dialogue thrives. By strengthening trust and transparency, leadership enhances systemic coherence. With leadership redefined, attention now turns to technological alignment.

CHAPTER . 22

Designing Ethical Systems

Designing ethical systems requires embedding responsibility into the foundations of technology rather than attempting to correct harm after deployment. Ethical considerations must begin at the concept stage. When values guide architecture, outcomes are more likely to align with human well-being. Reactive fixes are less effective than proactive design. Preventative ethics reduces unintended consequences. Structure shapes behavior.

An ethical system prioritizes transparency. Users should understand how data is collected, processed, and utilized. Clear explanations strengthen informed consent. When processes are visible, accountability increases. Accountability discourages misuse. Visibility builds trust between creators and users.

Equity is another core principle in ethical design. Systems should avoid reinforcing existing inequalities. Bias can emerge unintentionally through training data or algorithmic structure. Regular evaluation helps identify disparities. Continuous auditing supports fairness. Fairness sustains legitimacy over time.

Human-centered design ensures that technology serves users rather than dominating them. Tools should enhance autonomy and capability. Interfaces must be intuitive and accessible. Accessibility expands inclusion across diverse populations. Inclusive design strengthens societal participation. Participation improves collective outcomes.

Ethical systems also incorporate feedback mechanisms. Monitoring real-world impact allows for adjustments. Adaptive improvement ensures alignment with evolving needs. Responsiveness prevents stagnation. Iterative refinement strengthens reliability. Continuous evaluation reinforces accountability.

When ethical principles are integrated into system design, technology becomes a stabilizing force rather than a destabilizing one. Responsible architecture amplifies clarity and cooperation. By embedding transparency, equity, and accountability into technological foundations, societies can reduce systemic risk. Ethical alignment transforms innovation into long-term benefit. With design principles established, attention shifts to algorithmic responsibility.

CHAPTER . 23

Algorithmic Responsibility

Algorithmic responsibility requires that the creators and operators of automated systems acknowledge their influence on information flow and public perception. Algorithms determine what content is prioritized, recommended, or suppressed. These choices shape attention patterns at scale. Because of this influence, design decisions carry social consequences. Responsibility must therefore accompany deployment. Impact should be anticipated, measured, and refined.

Transparency is central to algorithmic responsibility. Users should understand the general principles guiding content selection. While proprietary details may remain protected, clear explanations of objectives and ranking factors improve trust. Visibility into system goals reduces suspicion. When people comprehend how recommendations function, they can engage more critically. Understanding strengthens autonomy.

Regular auditing is another essential component. Independent reviews help identify unintended bias or harmful outcomes. Audits assess whether systems disproportionately amplify certain types of content. Evaluation processes should include diverse stakeholders. Continuous monitoring ensures that adjustments can be made promptly. Iterative correction reduces long-term harm.

Design choices must consider societal effects, not only technical performance. Optimization for engagement alone can unintentionally prioritize sensational material. Broader metrics should include credibility, diversity of perspective, and constructive contribution. Balanced evaluation frameworks support healthier ecosystems. When performance indicators reflect social value, incentives shift accordingly. Incentives guide behavior.

User control mechanisms enhance algorithmic accountability. Providing customization options allows individuals to influence their information environment. Adjustable settings empower users to shape exposure levels. Control over recommendation intensity improves personal agency. Agency supports informed participation. Empowered users contribute to system stability.

Algorithmic responsibility transforms automated systems from passive tools into accountable participants in information ecosystems. When transparency, auditing, and user control are integrated, trust improves. Responsible algorithms can support clarity rather than distortion. Ethical alignment strengthens collective understanding. With responsibility established, the next focus is building information verification ecosystems.

CHAPTER . 24

Information Verification Ecosystems

Information verification ecosystems are interconnected networks of tools, institutions, and practices designed to confirm accuracy before content spreads widely. In environments where information travels instantly, verification must operate with similar efficiency. Without structured validation, errors can propagate rapidly. Ecosystems of verification slow misinformation through layered review. Multiple checkpoints increase reliability. Reliability strengthens public confidence.

Effective verification begins with source transparency. Content should clearly indicate origin and authorship. Knowing who created information allows for contextual evaluation. Traceable sources enable accountability. Accountability discourages manipulation. Clear provenance supports trust.

Cross-referencing is another foundational practice. Independent confirmation from credible references reduces the likelihood of error. When multiple reliable sources align, confidence increases. Discrepancies signal the need for further review. Structured comparison improves accuracy. Accuracy reduces confusion.

Technology can enhance verification processes. Automated fact-checking tools can flag inconsistencies for human review. However, human oversight remains essential for contextual judgment. Combining computational speed with expert evaluation strengthens outcomes. Hybrid systems balance efficiency and discernment. Integration improves effectiveness.

Educational components are equally important within verification ecosystems. Media literacy training equips individuals to evaluate claims critically. Understanding logical fallacies and bias detection strengthens analysis. Informed users contribute to system-wide accuracy. Collective competence reduces dependence on centralized correction. Shared skill increases resilience.

Verification ecosystems function best when collaboration exists among platforms, institutions, and communities. Shared standards promote interoperability. When evaluation criteria align, corrections spread more efficiently. Coordinated responses prevent duplication of effort. Cooperation enhances consistency. With verification frameworks reinforced, attention turns toward human-centered innovation.

CHAPTER . 25

Human-Centered Innovation

Human-centered innovation prioritizes human well-being, dignity, and long-term benefit as the primary measures of technological progress. Innovation should enhance capabilities without undermining autonomy. When development focuses solely on efficiency or profit, unintended consequences may arise. By placing people at the core of design decisions, systems become more aligned with societal needs. Purpose-driven innovation strengthens sustainability. Sustainability ensures enduring value.

User experience must reflect accessibility and inclusivity. Technologies should be usable across diverse abilities, backgrounds, and contexts. Simplified interfaces reduce barriers to entry. Clear design improves comprehension and reduces misuse. Accessibility expands participation in digital ecosystems. Participation increases collective benefit.

Human-centered innovation also evaluates long-term impact. Short-term performance metrics may overlook cumulative effects. Responsible development includes lifecycle assessment and continuous monitoring. Feedback from real users informs refinement. Iterative improvement supports adaptation. Adaptation ensures relevance across changing conditions.

Ethical review processes contribute to human-centered outcomes. Cross-disciplinary teams can assess technical proposals for social implications. Including diverse perspectives reduces blind spots.

Structured evaluation identifies potential risks early. Early detection allows preventive adjustments. Prevention is more effective than remediation.

Innovation should amplify human strengths rather than replace essential human judgment. Automation can assist decision-making, but oversight remains necessary. Collaboration between human insight and technological tools yields balanced results. Systems that enhance reasoning support better outcomes. Enhancement increases collective capability. Capability strengthens resilience.

When innovation aligns with human-centered principles, technology becomes a partner in progress rather than a destabilizing force. Design choices shape cultural trajectories. By centering dignity, transparency, and inclusion, development fosters trust. Trust enables adoption and cooperation. With innovation grounded in human priorities, attention turns toward data with context.

CHAPTER . 26

Data with Context

Data alone is incomplete without interpretation. Numbers, metrics, and statistics provide valuable signals, but they require framing to become meaningful. When data is presented without context, it can lead to misunderstanding. Context explains conditions, limitations, and methods of collection. It clarifies what the data represents and what it does not. Understanding depends on interpretation as much as measurement.

Raw data can appear objective, yet its meaning depends on structure. Sampling methods, timing, and definitions influence outcomes. Without awareness of these factors, conclusions may be inaccurate. Transparent methodology strengthens credibility. Clear explanation reduces misapplication. Context transforms information into insight.

Providing context improves decision-making. Leaders and citizens alike benefit from understanding how figures were generated. When assumptions are visible, evaluation becomes more accurate. Documentation of sources and procedures enhances reliability. Reliable interpretation supports responsible action. Responsible action builds trust.

Context also includes historical and environmental background. Trends cannot be understood by isolated snapshots alone. Longitudinal analysis reveals patterns over time. Comparing data across relevant periods increases clarity. Awareness of broader conditions prevents overgeneralization. Broader perspective strengthens judgment.

Educational systems should emphasize contextual thinking. Teaching individuals how to interpret charts, reports, and research findings reduces misinterpretation. Critical evaluation skills improve analytical depth. When learners understand methodology, they become more discerning consumers of information. Discernment strengthens resilience against distortion. Informed interpretation supports social stability.

Data with context ensures that information serves understanding rather than confusion. By pairing quantitative evidence with clear explanation, systems enhance transparency. Contextualized data promotes responsible communication. It reduces the likelihood of manipulation through selective presentation. Clarity in framing strengthens shared comprehension. With context integrated into information systems, the focus now shifts to resilient digital communities.

CHAPTER . 27

Resilient Digital Communities

Resilient digital communities are online environments designed to support constructive interaction, shared learning, and long-term stability. In many current systems, engagement is prioritized over well-being. Resilience requires shifting emphasis toward safety, clarity, and mutual respect. When communities are structured around these principles, participation becomes healthier. Stability increases when norms are clearly defined. Clear norms reduce confusion and conflict.

Strong digital communities establish transparent guidelines. Codes of conduct define acceptable behavior and outline consequences for violations. Predictable enforcement builds trust among participants. Consistency in moderation prevents perceptions of bias. Fair procedures encourage ongoing engagement. Engagement thrives when participants feel protected.

Community resilience also depends on inclusive participation. Platforms should reduce barriers that limit access or expression. Accessibility features expand opportunities for diverse users. When many voices contribute constructively, discussions become richer. Diversity strengthens collective intelligence. Broad participation improves problem-solving capacity.

Conflict management mechanisms are essential in digital spaces. Structured mediation processes help resolve disputes before escalation. Clear reporting systems enable timely intervention. Early response reduces long-term disruption. Restorative approaches repair relationships rather than simply punishing misconduct. Repair supports continuity and cooperation.

Resilient communities encourage constructive content rather than reactive amplification. Systems can promote educational resources, collaborative projects, and evidence-based discussions. Highlighting positive contributions reinforces desired behavior. Recognition of valuable input shapes community culture. Culture influences future participation. Intentional reinforcement guides norms.

By combining transparent governance, inclusive access, and restorative practices, digital environments can become stable spaces for dialogue and collaboration. Resilience does not mean eliminating disagreement; it means managing it effectively. Structured environments reduce volatility. Predictability increases confidence. With resilient communities established, the next focus is technology as an amplifier of wisdom.

Chapter . 28

Technology as Amplifier of Wisdom

Technology becomes an amplifier of wisdom when it enhances human understanding, ethical reasoning, and cooperative capacity rather than merely increasing speed or scale. Tools are not inherently beneficial or harmful; their impact depends on design and application. When aligned with thoughtful principles, technology can extend insight across communities. It can distribute knowledge efficiently. It can strengthen shared learning. Alignment determines outcome.

Wisdom requires reflection, context, and long-term perspective. Technological systems that encourage pause and evaluation support better judgment. Features such as source transparency, context labeling, and verification prompts can improve decision quality. By integrating reflective mechanisms, platforms can reduce impulsive reactions. Reflection enhances discernment. Discernment supports stability.

Collaborative tools also contribute to wisdom amplification. Shared workspaces, open research repositories, and communication platforms enable collective problem-solving. When information flows responsibly between participants, innovation accelerates constructively. Structured cooperation reduces duplication and fragmentation. Coordination strengthens outcomes. Shared effort multiplies effectiveness.

Education-focused technologies further extend wisdom. Adaptive learning systems can provide personalized instruction while maintaining ethical standards. Access to reliable educational resources expands opportunity. Knowledge distribution reduces inequality of information. Informed populations are better equipped to evaluate claims. Education reinforces resilience.

However, amplification must be guided by accountability. Without oversight, technology can amplify distortion as easily as clarity. Responsible governance ensures alignment with societal values. Continuous evaluation identifies unintended effects. Feedback-driven refinement maintains balance. Accountability sustains trust.

When technology is intentionally designed to elevate understanding, it becomes a stabilizing force in complex systems. It can connect expertise, verify information, and distribute insight widely. By prioritizing ethical alignment and transparency, innovation strengthens collective intelligence. Wisdom scales when systems are structured thoughtfully. With technological alignment addressed, the next section turns toward economic and structural renewal.

CHAPTER . 29

Sustainable Economic Indicators

Sustainable economic indicators expand the definition of success beyond short-term financial gain. Traditional metrics often emphasize growth rates and quarterly performance. While these measures provide useful information, they do not fully capture long-term societal health. Broader indicators incorporate environmental stability, social well-being, and resource resilience. When measurement systems evolve, incentives shift accordingly. Incentives shape outcomes.

Economic health should reflect durability as well as expansion. A system that grows rapidly but depletes essential resources is not truly stable. Long-term indicators account for ecological impact and regenerative capacity. Tracking these dimensions helps prevent hidden costs. Transparent measurement reduces unintended consequences. Comprehensive evaluation improves strategic planning.

Social indicators are equally important. Metrics related to education access, public health, and community trust provide insight into collective well-being. When societies invest in human capital, future productivity increases. Measuring opportunity and equity strengthens fairness. Fairness supports stability. Stability enhances economic confidence.

Environmental indicators measure sustainability of natural systems. Resource consumption, emissions levels, and biodiversity trends reveal ecological impact. Integrating these data points into economic reporting encourages responsible behavior. Decision-makers can then balance growth with conservation. Balance reduces systemic risk. Risk reduction improves resilience.

Alternative indicator frameworks require collaboration across sectors. Governments, businesses, and communities must agree on shared measurement standards. Consistent data collection enables comparison and accountability. Transparency in reporting strengthens credibility. Credibility fosters trust in institutions. Trust encourages long-term cooperation.

When economic success includes sustainability, societies align present activity with future viability. Broader metrics encourage innovation that protects resources while supporting prosperity. By redefining progress, systems can promote both stability and opportunity. Measurement influences motivation. With sustainable indicators established, attention turns to incentive redesign.

CHAPTER . 30

Incentive Redesign

Incentive redesign focuses on aligning reward structures with long-term human and environmental well-being. Systems naturally evolve toward what they reward. When incentives prioritize short-term gains, behavior follows that direction. To change outcomes, the underlying reward mechanisms must change. Structural adjustments influence collective patterns. Patterns determine results.

Many modern systems reward speed, scale, and engagement. While these qualities can drive innovation, they can also encourage harmful externalities if left unchecked. Redesigning incentives involves incorporating sustainability and accountability into evaluation criteria. Performance metrics should reflect ethical and long-term considerations. Balanced evaluation encourages responsible behavior. Responsibility strengthens system integrity.

Financial incentives can be adjusted to favor durable outcomes. Investments that support resilience, regeneration, and stability can receive preferential treatment. Long-term value creation should be recognized alongside immediate returns. By incorporating extended time horizons, institutions encourage strategic thinking. Strategic thinking reduces volatility. Reduced volatility enhances confidence.

Non-financial incentives are equally influential. Recognition, reputation, and leadership opportunities shape motivation. Public acknowledgment of constructive contributions can guide behavior positively. Social rewards reinforce desired norms. Norms influence culture. Culture shapes everyday decisions.

Transparent evaluation systems improve incentive alignment. When criteria are clear, participants understand expectations. Clarity reduces ambiguity and gaming of metrics. Accountability mechanisms ensure fairness. Fairness sustains participation. Participation strengthens collective engagement.

Redesigning incentives is not about limiting ambition but redirecting it. When achievement is measured by long-term benefit rather than immediate output alone, innovation becomes more sustainable. Systems that reward collaboration and responsibility encourage stability. Stability reduces systemic risk. With incentives aligned toward sustainability, the focus moves to circular resource systems.

CHAPTER . 31

Circular Resource Systems

Circular resource systems are designed to minimize waste by keeping materials in continuous cycles of use, reuse, and regeneration. Traditional linear models extract resources, produce goods, and discard remnants. This approach increases depletion and environmental strain over time. Circular systems reduce dependency on constant extraction. They prioritize restoration alongside consumption. Regeneration strengthens long-term stability.

In circular models, products are designed for durability and repairability. Extending product lifespan reduces waste generation. Components can be refurbished or repurposed instead of discarded. Design choices made at the outset determine recyclability. Planning for end-of-life recovery improves efficiency. Efficiency reduces resource pressure.

Recycling and reuse form core elements of circular economies. Materials are collected, processed, and reintroduced into production streams. Effective infrastructure supports separation and recovery. Public participation enhances collection success. When communities engage in recycling practices, outcomes improve. Collective action amplifies impact.

Energy systems can also adopt circular principles. Renewable sources reduce reliance on finite resources. Energy storage technologies help balance supply and demand. Integrating efficiency measures decreases overall consumption. Reduced waste lowers environmental footprint. Sustainable energy management supports resilience.

Businesses play a central role in implementing circular strategies. Supply chain transparency allows tracking of materials across stages. Companies can redesign processes to prioritize minimal waste generation. Collaboration across industries increases system-wide effectiveness. Shared standards encourage consistency. Consistency improves scalability.

Circular resource systems contribute to economic and ecological balance. By decoupling growth from excessive extraction, societies reduce long-term risk. Resource efficiency fosters innovation in materials science and logistics. When waste declines, environmental stress decreases. Stability improves across sectors. With circular systems established, attention turns to equitable opportunity frameworks.

Chapter . 32

Equitable Opportunity Frameworks

Equitable opportunity frameworks ensure that access to education, employment, resources, and participation is not determined solely by circumstance or background. When opportunities are distributed unevenly, social mobility declines. Limited mobility restricts talent development. Societies benefit when individuals can contribute according to ability rather than starting position. Expanding access increases collective potential. Potential strengthens long-term prosperity.

Education is a foundational component of opportunity. High-quality learning environments enable skill development and critical thinking. When educational systems are inclusive, more individuals gain tools for advancement. Accessibility includes affordability, infrastructure, and supportive resources. Removing barriers expands participation. Participation enhances innovation.

Economic opportunity depends on fair access to capital, training, and markets. Support mechanisms such as small business development programs can foster entrepreneurship. Transparent hiring practices reduce bias. Merit-based evaluation aligned with clear standards promotes confidence. Fair processes strengthen trust. Trust encourages engagement.

Healthcare access also influences opportunity. Physical and mental well-being affect productivity and quality of life. Preventive care reduces long-term costs. Healthy populations contribute more effectively to economic and social systems. Equitable healthcare improves overall resilience. Resilience reduces systemic strain.

Digital inclusion is increasingly essential. Reliable internet access and technological literacy expand participation in modern economies. Providing infrastructure in underserved areas reduces disparities. Training programs can improve digital competence. Equal access to information tools enhances competitiveness. Competitiveness fosters innovation.

Equitable opportunity frameworks do not eliminate differences in outcomes, but they ensure that pathways to advancement are open. By focusing on fairness in process rather than uniformity in results, societies can maintain motivation and diversity. Inclusive systems strengthen cohesion. Cohesion supports stability. With opportunity frameworks reinforced, attention shifts toward localized resilience networks.

CHAPTER . 33

Localized Resilience Networks

Localized resilience networks strengthen communities by building capacity at regional and neighborhood levels. When essential systems are concentrated in distant or centralized structures, disruptions can have widespread effects. Local resilience reduces dependency on fragile supply chains. It distributes resources and capabilities more evenly. Decentralization improves adaptability. Adaptability supports stability during uncertainty.

Resilience begins with strong local infrastructure. Reliable energy, water, transportation, and communication systems form the backbone of community continuity. Investing in maintenance and modernization reduces vulnerability to shocks. Preventative upgrades are more cost-effective than emergency recovery. Prepared systems respond more effectively to disruption. Preparation enhances confidence.

Community partnerships are central to resilience networks. Collaboration between public institutions, private organizations, and civic groups strengthens coordination. Shared planning improves alignment of resources and responsibilities. Clear communication channels support rapid response. Cooperation reduces duplication of effort. Coordination increases efficiency.

Local food systems contribute significantly to resilience. Supporting regional agriculture reduces reliance on distant supply chains. Community-supported initiatives can enhance food security. Diversified production methods improve stability. Sustainable practices protect soil and ecosystems. Food security strengthens overall well-being.

Training and skill-sharing programs further reinforce networks. When community members possess diverse competencies, they can respond flexibly to challenges. Knowledge exchange strengthens collective problem-solving. Local workshops and collaborative projects enhance preparedness. Skill development increases self-reliance. Self-reliance reduces systemic pressure.

Localized resilience does not isolate communities from broader systems. Instead, it creates a foundation of stability that supports global integration. Strong local units contribute to stronger national and international networks. Distributed strength improves overall endurance. With resilience networks established, attention turns to adaptive governance models.

CHAPTER . 34

Adaptive Governance Models

Adaptive governance models are designed to respond effectively to change, uncertainty, and emerging challenges. Traditional governance structures often rely on rigid procedures that can struggle to keep pace with rapid developments. Adaptive systems incorporate feedback, evaluation, and revision into their core design. Flexibility enables institutions to evolve without losing stability. Responsiveness improves long-term effectiveness. Evolution supports resilience.

Continuous feedback is essential for adaptive governance. Policies should be monitored to assess outcomes and unintended consequences. Data-driven evaluation allows timely adjustments. When results diverge from expectations, structured revision can occur. Iterative improvement strengthens performance. Learning-oriented governance reduces stagnation.

Transparency enhances adaptability. Clear communication about decision criteria and implementation processes builds public trust. When stakeholders understand how and why decisions are made, cooperation increases. Open reporting mechanisms improve accountability. Accountability encourages responsible leadership. Responsibility sustains legitimacy.

Inclusive participation strengthens adaptive capacity. Diverse input provides broader perspective on complex issues. Engaging multiple stakeholders increases awareness of local conditions.

Collaborative policy design improves practicality. Shared ownership of outcomes enhances commitment. Commitment improves policy implementation.

Technology can support adaptive governance through data analysis and communication platforms. Real-time information systems help leaders understand evolving trends. However, human judgment remains essential for contextual interpretation. Balancing automated insights with deliberative processes ensures ethical alignment. Integration of tools and expertise enhances decision quality. Balanced systems improve stability.

Adaptive governance models emphasize iteration rather than permanence. Policies are treated as living frameworks subject to refinement. This mindset encourages experimentation within accountable boundaries. Continuous improvement fosters institutional resilience. With governance systems capable of evolving, societies are better prepared for global integration.

CHAPTER . 35

Planetary Perspective

A planetary perspective recognizes that many of today's challenges extend beyond national borders and require coordinated global awareness. Environmental systems, economic networks, and digital infrastructures operate at interconnected scales. Actions taken in one region can produce effects elsewhere. Understanding this interdependence encourages broader responsibility. Shared awareness strengthens collective decision-making. Interconnection demands cooperation.

Climate stability is a clear example of planetary interdependence. Atmospheric changes influence agriculture, water systems, and public health across regions. Addressing such issues requires collaboration among nations and institutions. Isolated solutions are insufficient for global-scale dynamics. Cooperative frameworks improve effectiveness. Coordination reduces duplication and conflict.

Economic systems are similarly interconnected. Supply chains link producers and consumers across continents. Financial markets transmit signals rapidly between regions. Disruptions in one area can influence stability elsewhere. Recognizing these linkages supports strategic planning. Strategic awareness reduces systemic vulnerability.

Digital communication networks further integrate global societies. Information spreads instantly across time zones and cultures. This connectivity enables collaboration and knowledge exchange. However, it also increases the potential for rapid misinformation. Responsible digital governance becomes essential. Shared standards improve reliability.

A planetary perspective does not diminish local identity or sovereignty. Instead, it complements them by adding a layer of global responsibility. Local action and global awareness can coexist productively. Decisions can be evaluated for both regional and planetary impact. Dual awareness strengthens sustainability. Sustainability ensures continuity.

By adopting a planetary outlook, societies expand their frame of reference beyond immediate boundaries. This broader vision encourages long-term stewardship of shared resources. It fosters collaboration rather than competition in addressing common challenges. When global awareness guides policy and innovation, cooperation becomes more achievable. With planetary perspective established, the focus shifts to cross-cultural signal exchange.

CHAPTER . 36

Cross-Cultural Signal Exchange

Cross-cultural signal exchange strengthens global understanding by promoting respectful sharing of knowledge, values, and practices across diverse societies. In a connected world, cultures interact continuously through travel, trade, media, and digital communication. These interactions create opportunities for mutual learning. When exchange is guided by respect, it builds bridges rather than barriers. Respectful dialogue reduces misunderstanding. Understanding enhances cooperation.

Effective cross-cultural exchange requires listening as much as speaking. Each culture carries unique historical experiences and contextual knowledge. Approaching differences with curiosity encourages constructive engagement. Assumptions can distort interpretation. Open inquiry fosters deeper insight. Insight supports collaboration.

Language clarity plays a significant role in cross-cultural communication. Translating ideas accurately preserves meaning. Simplified explanations can help bridge complexity without oversimplification. Shared terminology improves alignment. Precision in language reduces ambiguity. Reduced ambiguity minimizes conflict.

Cultural exchange benefits from recognizing common human values. While traditions may differ, many societies share commitments to well-being, fairness, and community. Identifying overlapping principles creates a foundation for partnership. Shared aspirations encourage joint initiatives. Common goals strengthen unity. Unity supports coordinated action.

Educational programs can support cross-cultural understanding. Learning about global histories, perspectives, and innovations broadens awareness. Exposure to diverse viewpoints increases adaptability. Intercultural competence strengthens professional and social interactions. Competence reduces friction in international collaboration. Collaboration accelerates progress.

Cross-cultural signal exchange does not require uniformity. Diversity enriches global systems by introducing varied approaches to problem-solving. When exchange occurs with humility and transparency, knowledge flows constructively. Mutual respect sustains long-term relationships. With exchange strengthened, attention turns toward conflict transformation systems.

Chapter . 37

Conflict Transformation Systems

Conflict transformation systems focus on addressing the underlying causes of disputes rather than merely managing surface-level disagreements. Conflict is a natural outcome of diverse interests, values, and perspectives. The goal is not to eliminate differences, but to channel them constructively. When systems are designed for transformation, tensions become opportunities for growth. Growth strengthens relationships. Strengthened relationships enhance stability.

Effective transformation begins with early intervention. Identifying issues before they escalate reduces harm and preserves trust. Structured mediation processes provide neutral environments for discussion. Skilled facilitators help clarify positions and interests. Clarity reduces misinterpretation. Reduced misinterpretation lowers escalation risk.

Restorative approaches emphasize repairing relationships rather than assigning blame alone. Accountability remains important, but it is paired with dialogue and resolution. Participants are encouraged to understand impact and responsibility. Constructive acknowledgment of harm enables reconciliation. Reconciliation rebuilds cooperation. Cooperation supports long-term continuity.

Clear communication frameworks support conflict transformation. Ground rules ensure respectful interaction. Equal speaking opportunities prevent dominance. Transparent procedures increase confidence in fairness. Fairness improves participation. Participation enhances legitimacy.

Data and evidence can also support transformation processes. Shared facts help establish common ground. When disputes involve misinformation, verification reduces confusion. Reliable information creates a stable foundation for negotiation. Stability allows focus on solutions. Solutions emerge more readily when clarity replaces ambiguity.

Conflict transformation systems are most effective when embedded in institutions, communities, and digital platforms. Training in negotiation, empathy, and systems thinking strengthens capacity for resolution. By integrating these principles, societies reduce polarization and foster collaboration. Constructive conflict management improves resilience. With transformation frameworks established, attention now shifts to education for signal literacy.

CHAPTER . 38

Education for Signal Literacy

Education for signal literacy equips individuals with the skills needed to distinguish reliable information from noise, distortion, and manipulation. In high-volume information environments, the ability to evaluate sources is essential. Signal literacy combines critical thinking, media analysis, and systems awareness. These competencies help learners interpret complex data responsibly. Informed evaluation strengthens decision-making. Strong decisions improve outcomes.

Critical thinking forms the foundation of signal literacy. Students learn to question assumptions, analyze arguments, and identify logical fallacies. Structured reasoning reduces susceptibility to misinformation. Evaluating evidence improves accuracy. Accuracy enhances trust in conclusions. Trust supports constructive dialogue.

Media literacy expands this foundation by teaching how information is produced and distributed. Understanding editorial processes, algorithmic amplification, and framing techniques clarifies how narratives are shaped. Awareness of these mechanisms reduces passive consumption. Active engagement encourages verification. Verification limits the spread of errors. Informed users contribute to healthier ecosystems.

Systems thinking adds a broader perspective. Complex challenges often involve interconnected variables. Recognizing relationships between economic, environmental, and social factors improves comprehension. Viewing issues in isolation can lead to incomplete solutions. Holistic analysis strengthens policy development. Comprehensive understanding reduces unintended consequences.

Signal literacy education should also include emotional awareness. Emotional reactions can influence interpretation of information. Learning to recognize and regulate responses improves clarity. Balanced emotional processing supports rational evaluation. Stability enhances resilience under pressure. Resilience improves adaptability.

When education systems prioritize signal literacy, societies become more resistant to confusion and manipulation. Individuals gain confidence in navigating information landscapes. Communities benefit from shared analytical standards. Collective competence reduces polarization. With signal literacy integrated into education, attention turns toward intergenerational alignment.

CHAPTER . 39

Intergenerational Alignment

Intergenerational alignment ensures that present decisions account for the well-being of future generations. Many modern challenges unfold over long time horizons. Environmental, economic, and technological choices made today will shape outcomes decades from now. Without deliberate consideration, short-term priorities can overshadow long-term consequences. Alignment introduces continuity into decision-making. Continuity strengthens sustainability.

Long-term planning requires structured foresight. Scenario analysis helps anticipate potential futures. By evaluating multiple possibilities, institutions can reduce vulnerability to uncertainty. Forward-looking policies incorporate adaptability. Adaptability allows systems to respond without sacrificing foundational stability. Stability benefits both current and future populations.

Education plays a central role in intergenerational responsibility. Teaching stewardship encourages awareness of legacy and impact. Students who understand long-term consequences are more likely to value sustainability. Generational perspective broadens ethical awareness. Ethical awareness improves collective judgment. Improved judgment supports durable progress.

Economic strategies should reflect intergenerational thinking. Investments in infrastructure, research, and environmental restoration create lasting value. Resource management must balance present use with future availability. Sustainable financing models can support extended timelines. Long-term returns often exceed immediate gains when stability is preserved. Stability increases confidence across generations.

Environmental stewardship is a key component of alignment. Preserving ecosystems protects biodiversity and natural resources. Responsible consumption reduces strain on planetary systems. Conservation efforts contribute to resilience. Resilience ensures that future communities inherit viable conditions. Viable conditions enable continued development.

Intergenerational alignment reframes progress as a continuous relay rather than a single moment. Each generation passes forward resources, knowledge, and responsibilities. When stewardship becomes a shared cultural value, decisions naturally incorporate long-term perspective. Alignment fosters continuity, accountability, and hope. With this principle established, the book moves toward its culminating vision.

CHAPTER . 40

The Ninth Horizon Vision

The Ninth Horizon Vision represents the synthesis of clarity, cooperation, resilience, and long-term alignment developed throughout this framework. It is not a destination but an ongoing orientation toward higher-order signal in a complex world. The horizon symbolizes forward awareness, where decisions are guided by both present realities and future consequences. By integrating internal clarity with systemic reform, societies can move toward sustained coherence. Vision provides direction. Direction enables progress.

At its core, the Ninth Horizon Vision restores signal across multiple dimensions of life. Personal discipline strengthens attention and emotional regulation. Transparent communication rebuilds trust within institutions. Ethical technology design reduces distortion. Sustainable economic indicators align incentives with long-term outcomes. Each domain contributes to a unified structure. Unity increases stability.

This vision emphasizes integration rather than fragmentation. Individual development supports social renewal. Social trust reinforces economic resilience. Technological responsibility enhances informational clarity. Environmental stewardship ensures planetary continuity. When these elements function together, systems reinforce one another. Reinforcement strengthens durability.

The Ninth Horizon is defined by shared responsibility. It recognizes that challenges are interconnected and require coordinated responses. Leadership becomes stewardship. Innovation becomes service. Governance becomes adaptive guidance. Communities become active participants in shaping outcomes. Collective engagement transforms complexity into opportunity.

Progress within this vision is measured by coherence rather than noise. Success is reflected in clarity of information, fairness of systems, and sustainability of resources. Conflict becomes a process for transformation rather than division. Education builds signal literacy. Technology amplifies wisdom. When these components align, societies regain stable direction. Stability supports creativity and growth.

The Signal from the Ninth Horizon ultimately calls for conscious evolution. It invites individuals, institutions, and nations to prioritize truth, cooperation, and long-term thinking. By restoring internal balance and external integrity, humanity can navigate complexity with confidence. The horizon remains forward, guiding continuous improvement. With clarity restored, the journey continues beyond this book into action.

Epilog

The journey toward clarity does not end with a book. It begins with application.

The systems described in these pages are not distant abstractions. They exist in daily choices — in what we consume, how we communicate, how we lead, how we design, and how we engage with others. Every interaction either strengthens signal or amplifies noise. Every decision contributes to the larger architecture of culture.

Restoring signal is not about retreating from complexity. It is about navigating complexity with awareness. It is about building technologies that serve humanity. It is about creating economies that value sustainability. It is about cultivating communities that prioritize trust. It is about designing leadership models rooted in integrity.

The Ninth Horizon is not a fixed endpoint. It is an ongoing orientation toward better systems and clearer intentions. When individuals commit to inner clarity, institutions respond. When communities demand transparency, governance evolves. When creativity aligns with responsibility, innovation becomes constructive.

The future will always contain uncertainty. But uncertainty does not require confusion. With stronger signal, humanity can move forward with confidence — not because the world is simple, but because we are prepared.

The horizon remains open.

About the Author

Laura Lee is a writer, creative entrepreneur, and digital visionary whose work explores the intersection of clarity, innovation, and conscious design. Raised in a quiet town where storytelling served as connection and survival, she discovered early that expression has the power to shape identity, community, and opportunity.

As the founder of a successful digital design agency, Laura has partnered with organizations and brands to develop identities grounded in purpose, coherence, and authenticity. Her work emphasizes that design is not merely visual — it is structural. It influences behavior, communication, and perception. Through strategy, branding, and digital architecture, she helps build systems that reflect intention rather than noise.

Her writing extends these principles into broader cultural conversations. Whether addressing personal growth, creative empowerment, or systemic transformation, her themes remain consistent: authenticity, healing, responsibility, and conscious creation. She believes clarity is a form of leadership, and integrity is a form of innovation.

Through her books, digital platforms, and consulting work, Laura empowers individuals and organizations to articulate their values, refine their voice, and build structures aligned with long-term vision. She approaches creativity as a tool for alignment — where emotion and strategy, beauty and functionality, heart and system coexist.

Signal from the Ninth Horizon is an extension of that mission — a framework for restoring clarity in complex environments and building a future guided by intention, coherence, and hope.

www.ingramcontent.com/pod-product-compliance
Lightning Source LLC
LaVergne TN
LVHW022115200926
848481LV00003B/1174